Teenagers and Peer Pressure

by
Stephen Douglas Williford

13 Biblical Lessons Especially for Teenagers with Practical Applications for Everyday Problems

QUALITY PUBLICATIONS
P.O. BOX 1060
ABILENE, TEXAS 79604

© Stephen Douglas Williford

1984

All rights reserved. No part of this publication may be reproduced, stored in a retrieval system, or transmitted in any form by any means — electronic, mechanical, photocopy, recording, or otherwise — without prior permission of the copyright owner.

ISBN: 0-89137-809-X

Dedication

This book is dedicated to those two people who gave me the examples of what a Christian should be. My Mother and Father. Mother taught in at least a million Vacation Bible Schools and always welcomed the pew of visitors I invited. Somehow she managed to squeeze all of them in our '55 Buick. She read Cindy and me Bible story after Bible story and taught our Bible school classes as we grew up.

Daddy taught junior high, senior high, drove camp buses and hay ride trucks and enjoyed every minute of it. Mother and Daddy took teaching seriously. They spent hours each week working on their lessons. They encouraged me in my Christian growth. I can remember making a short talk in church while I was still in high school. Daddy came up afterwards and beamed, "What you did makes me more proud than anything a person could do in athletics." That meant a lot since he was an athlete and I sat on the bench, no matter how hard I tried. I can remember the countless times Mother visited the sick and saddened, often being one of many and sometimes being one of the few who came.

Mother and Daddy provided me with a Christian education, from elementary school to college and I never heard them complain about the financial burden it had to be. They showed me what Christianity was all about, in the classroom and out. Through their love, patience and support, I was able to deal with problems much more effectively.

So, this is dedicated to my Mother and Daddy. You might say, they wrote it.

Dedicated to
Henry and Irma Williford

Teacher's Page

Welcome to *Teenagers and Peer Pressure!* You will find 13 biblical lessons for teens with very practical applications to their everyday struggles. The lessons are divided into four sections:

Looking Inward   Lessons 1-3
Looking Outward   Lessons 4-6
Looking Upward   Lessons 7-11
Looking for Others   Lessons 12-13

Unless noted, each lesson follows the same format:
1) Scripture reading
2) Reading and Exercises in book
3) Class or Group Discussion
4) Project or Application

Each lesson is designed to center in on a biblical truth that can be directly applied to a teen's problems. Such problems throughout the 13-lesson study will include: dating, drugs and alcohol, self-image, parent-teen life, friendships, peer pressure and evangelism.

Several of the lessons are designed for small group discussion. These are groups of 3-8 people which at least initially need to have an adult group leader. Guidelines for groups should include:
a) Everyone gets an opportunity to speak.
b) No one should dominate the discussion.
c) Start the first groups by going around a circle and asking each each person, "What do you think?"
d) Groups should have different people in them each week.

These lessons were designed to be both biblical and practical. I wanted to enable the students to see that God can answer their problems. Some thoughts are repeated for emphasis throughout the lessons.

Let me encourage you to let your imagination and creativity go to work for you as you prepare for these lessons. I hope that you will grow to look forward to the biblical truths you will teach your class each week. May God bless your work!

Stephen Douglas Williford

Table of Contents

Looking Inward

Lesson 1 Moses 6
Lesson 2 The Lazy Servant 10
Lesson 3 The Woman Caught in Adultery 14

Looking Outward

Lesson 4 Noah 18
Lesson 5 The Prodigal Son 23
Lesson 6 The Golden Rule in Dating 27

Looking Upward

Lesson 7   Daniel and the Lions' Den 35
Lesson 8   Joseph: Trusting in God 39
Lesson 9   Shadrach, Meshach and Abednego 44
Lesson 10 Job 49
Lesson 11 The Rich Young Ruler 53

Looking for Others

Lesson 12 The Good Samaritan 56
Lesson 13 The Salt of the Earth 61

1

Moses

Scripture: Exodus 3:1-4:17

Moses was tending sheep by the mountain Horeb when he saw this bush that kept burning and burning but would not burn up. Moses decided to go inspect this unusual sight. As he got closer, a voice from *inside the bush* called his name!

Can you imagine being in Moses' place? There he is in a desert and hears his name being called from a bush that will not burn up. What would you do? _____

Moses replied with "Here I am."

As you know, God was speaking and said He had picked Moses to deliver the Israelites out of Egypt. Now that might not seem like much to you and me because we have read about the story of Moses and the burning bush for years. But Moses was hearing and seeing this for the *first time!* Furthermore, God wanted Moses, who had killed an Egyptian in Egypt, to go back to Egypt, the most powerful nation in the world at the time and tell its ruler, "I'm here to pick up the Israelites."

Moses' first response was, "*Who am I* to deliver the Israelites?" Moses understood that God was talking about a BIG job and said, "Listen, I'm a *nobody*. I can't do it." Does that sound familiar? Are there times when you feel like a nobody? _____ If so, when? _____

What was God's reply to Moses? _____

Moses' second response to God was, "What if they ask, 'What's the name of the God that sent you?'" God instructed Moses to say, "I AM has sent me to you."

Moses' third response was, "What if they don't take me seriously?" God turned Moses' staff into a snake. It scared Moses to death and he ran! Then God told him to pick it up by its tail and it turned back into his staff.

This had been some day for Moses. First, a burning bush that would not burn up, then God Himself speaking to Moses from within that bush, and now a snake out of a staff. But that wasn't all. God told Moses to put his hand in his coat. When he pulled it out, it was leprous (very diseased). Can you imagine how Moses felt? God restored his hand and said if they still did not believe, Moses could turn some water into blood.

After all of this, what would your response have been to God? _____

Moses' fourth response was, "But I'm a poor speaker." God said He could help since He had made his mouth.

Moses' final response was, "Please send someone else!" Moses thought of other people more capable than he was. He knew the weaknesses that he had. So he asked God to pick another. This made God angry. Why do you think God was mad? _____

Before we criticize Moses too quickly, his final response is familiar, isn't it? Haven't you had similar thoughts such as: "I'm not smart enought to do that," or "I'm not cute enough to go out with him," or "She wouldn't want to go out with me," or "I could never teach that class," or "They'd never want me to be their friend."

How are you like Moses in saying, "Send someone else"? ___

Moses did not think too much of himself. He did not believe he was capable of handling God's will for his life. If you were standing there at the burning bush with Moses, what would you say to encourage him? _____

For Moses, going back into Egypt was very hard to trust God with. What is hard for you to trust God with?_____
_____

God has created you differently from anyone alse who has ever been and who ever will be. Just like He did Moses. He requires much of you too, just like Moses. Sometimes you might look in the mirror and say, "How could God need anything from *me*?" That is the exact same way Moses felt!

Sally *really* wanted to go on the church retreat, but was afraid she would not have a good time. She was afraid no one would want to spend time with her. What would you tell Sally? _____
_____

God told Moses to trust Him. Name at least three reasons why *you* should trust God.
1)_____
2)_____
3)_____

Moses felt he was a nobody. Name three reasons why you should value yourself.
1)_____
2)_____ _____
3)_____
What does trust in God have to do with liking yourself? ____
_____

Draw a heart on butcher paper or a poster board and combine the reasons the class wrote for why you should value yourself.

God's message to Moses was "TRUST ME!" and Moses kept saying, "I'm a nobody." God's message is the same for you today. He is not in a burning bush and your pencil is probably not going to become a snake, but He *IS* saying it just as plainly to you as He did to Moses. And He is just as interested in your reply.

Teacher instructions: Perhaps you will want each of the students to bring a school photograph to place in the drawing or you could take a polaroid photo of the entire group. You will need some butcher paper or a poster board, some tape and a magic marker or crayon.

2

The Lazy Servant

Scripture: Matthew 25:14-30

You know the parable of the talents. The master was about to take a trip. But before he left, he gave his three servants some coins called talents. Two of the servants used their coins to produce more coins. But the other servant, who was only given one talent, buried his coin.

I wonder what life was like for these three servants during these days. We are not told what servants 1 and 2 did with their coins, but we are told they used them to make more money. I imagine they had to work at it every day. This was a real test for them. After all, the master was miles away and probably was not coming home for awhile. It would have been easy to goof off. But they worked as if the master was still there.

The third servant had a different strategy. He buried his coin. I wonder what his thoughts were during these days? Perhaps they were similar to these: "Sure, it's *easy* for those two to take a chance with the master's money. He gave them more than one coin. But I only have one coin to lose. *If* I had *their money*, I'd be working too. Besides, the boss can't expect much from me since he only gave me this one talent."

Have you ever thought about what that servant *did* while his fellow servants were earning money with their coins? He buried his coin so he could not use it to make more money. Perhaps he slept under a shade tree. Perhaps he tried to persuade the other two to quit. However he spent it, he wasted his time and the responsibility the master gave him.

Then, the master returned and asked the servants how they did with his money. The first and second servants showed him they had doubled what he gave them. He told them that they did a good job and he was proud of them. Then he faced the third servant who gave him back the same coin the master earlier had given him. The servant explained he was afraid he would lose it if he attempted to use it to make more money. The master was furious! He took his coin and gave it to the servant with ten talents and threw the servant out.

What application does this parable have to *your* life? _____
_____
_____

Why was the master so upset? _____
_____

I think this parable has a lot to say about *you*. You are one of those three servants. God has entrusted a life to you filled with abilities and opportunities. The question is, *How are you using it?* Are you saying, "If only I were more like him (or her), then I could do a lot more"? There will always be someone who is more intelligent, more attractive, more popular, more talented, more talkative and more secure than you are. It is very easy to compare your life with theirs and decide you are not worth much. It is also easy to make excuses for why you cannot serve God. Which servant are you? _____

Why? _____

Pretend you are the third servant who buried his money. The master has given you five minutes to explain your actions. How will you respond? _____

The master expected his servants to use what he had given them. God expects the same of you. God expects you to use what He has given you. The master was not interested in the third servant's excuses. He knew the servant was capable and was angry for the servant's doubt in himself. You can probably think of a situation in which you doubted your worth. Why is it easy to feel like the third servant? _____

What does God say to your self-doubt? _____

Name a few abilities and opportunities God has blessed you with:
1) _____
2) _____
3) _____

How does the way you feel about yourself affect your ability to serve God? _____

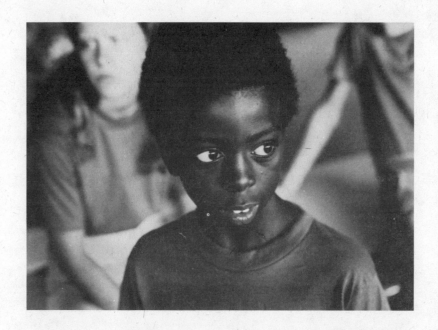

Each person should take a grocery sack and write his/her name on it. Next, write how *each* person in the room encourages you or what you appreciate about him/her. After you finish, go around and drop your note in that person's sack.

Teacher instructions: Bring enough grocery sacks for each person to have one. Bring enough paper for class members to write a separate note about each member of the class. You will also need pencils, pens and magic markers or crayons for the sacks.

3
The Woman Caught in Adultery

Scriptures: John 3:16; Romans 5:6-11; 8:1,2,31-38

Put John 3:16 into your own words. _____
_____

Put Romans 5:6-11 into your own words. _____
_____
_____

Put Romans 8:1,2,31-38 into your own words. _____
_____
_____

How does God see you? _____
_____

How does God want you to see yourself? _____
_____

Why is it important to value yourself? _____
_____
_____

Have you ever felt like a goldfish? Ever feel like *everyone* is looking at you? That they notice that hair out of place, the pimple behind your ear or remember that you had worn that shirt eight days ago? How do you handle it? Perhaps you work a half hour on getting the right side of your hair to match the left side. Or maybe you spend a long time in front of the closet trying to figure out what to wear. Or it could be that you feel like you are on stage all the time and cannot act natural.

Angie felt like a goldfish. She did not like herself. She hated the way she looked and acted. She felt like no one could like her for who she was. What is wrong with Angie's thinking? ___
_____

Why might Angie be headed for trouble? _____
_____

What would you say to Angie? Share your answers with the class. _____
_____

Read John 8:1-11.

This woman had several reasons to dislike herself. There were a lot of people with stones in their hands who made it obvious that they did not like her. Jesus understood the scribes and Pharisees were using the woman's sins as a test for Him. Can you picture this dramatic scene? As Jesus is teaching the people in the temple, the scribes and Pharisees march in with this woman they said was caught in the act of adultery. They ask Jesus what to do with the woman.

The large room was probably completely silent, awaiting Jesus' reply to this difficult question. Jesus suggests that the person without sin pitch the first rock. When the crowd leaves, Jesus then tells the girl to go and sin no more. How do you think the woman felt? _____
_____

Jesus told the woman to go and sin no more. You have sinned many times in your life. Perhaps you feel guilty and ashamed over those mistakes. Is it hard to give up guilt? Explain. _____
_____
_____
_____

How will you control your life?

Questions Just for You

Below are a few questions designed for you to answer individually. Perhaps you will want to talk about your answers in your group discussion.

What do you control in your life? _____
_____

What do you have no control over in your life? _____
_____

Which of these affects your self-image the most? _____
_____

Why? _____
_____

Break into groups of three or four and discuss these questions:

1) How does the way God sees you affect the way you see yourself? _____
_____

2) How can the way God sees you help with peer pressure?
_____

3) Jesus says to us just as forcefully as He said to the woman that day in the temple, "Go and sin no more." How does that apply to us today? _____
_____

Teacher instructions: Perhaps you can bring in a goldfish and place him in the center of the class. The last exercise is designed for the class to do in small groups. If time permits, ask the groups to report on their discussion at the end of class.

4

Noah

Scripture: Genesis 6:5-7:16

Chances are, Noah is one of the first Bible stories you ever heard. It is very hard for us to place ourselves in Noah's position. Why? _____
_____

Noah was asked to do something no one else had ever done. No doubt he faced ridicule from his neighbors. He certainly was the talk of the neighborhood. Who else was building a boat larger than his house miles away from water?

Even though it is difficult, pretend you are Noah. How do you feel? _____
_____

Why? _____
_____

What type of man was Noah? _____
_____
_____

List three people you know who remind you of Noah.
1) _____
2) _____
3) _____

Divide into groups of three or four and share and explain your choices. Then reassemble and share some of your choices with the class.

Noah trusted in God while he received no support from his friends or neighbors. Can you think of others in the Bible who did the same? Name them and explain. _____
_____
_____
_____
_____

Give some situations in which you or a friend acted as a Christian and received no support for your faithfulness.
_____
_____
_____

How can friends help us serve the Lord?
_____
_____
_____

Is there such a thing as "positive peer pressure"? Please explain your answer. _____
_____
_____
_____

A good friend is:
_____
_____
_____

What are some ways that you try to be a good friend?
_____
_____
_____

For Noah, the ark was something he built for the Lord and was ridiculed for. Even though you will never physically build an ark, you have opportunities to do things for the Lord that leaves you open for ridicule. As a class, discuss some of these opportunities, write them on some paper arks, string them together with yarn and hang them by the ends of the yarn somewhere in the room.

Divide back into your groups and make up a situation that would provide plenty of ridicule and how you would handle it. Make this specific with fictional names and places. Summarize your situation in the space below:

_____
_____
_____
_____
_____
_____
_____

Complete the following situation: David had to decide whether to _____ or _____. His parents wanted him to __ _____ but his friends wanted to _____. His decision was a hard one because _____. He decided to _____ even though it would make _____ mad.

If time permits, share your situations with the rest of the class.

Teacher instructions: Ask the class not to be in the same groups as last time. Before class cut out some paper arks with a hole at the top. Also bring some yarn and magic markers or pens.

"Friendship and Term Papers"

The shadows of the trees in the front yard came through the office window and danced on my desk. I stared at my handwritten term paper - I pushed my chair back, shut my eyes and sighed loudly. I do that whenever I have a lot of work ahead of me. I had spent hours at the library staring at microfilm, pouring over reference books, and copying the essential information for my Psychology paper. I had spent more hours deciding how to put all that information into just the right format. And still I had to type it-all 12 pages of it. For some that might be easy, but for me... I'd rather take a beating. Oh, I had asked others to type it but they had other things going on, some legitimate reasons and others just excuses. Besides, who would be willing to type a paper the night before? That was a little too much to ask. Just then the door bell rang. I uncovered my eyes, quit sighing and opened the door. It was my friend, Tim Jordan.

"Mother said you've been trying to get in touch with me the last few days so I thought I'd come by and see what you wanted." Tim is a computer programmer and owner of an Apple II computer with a letter quality printer, which could type a term paper a lot quicker than I could...

"Well you may feel like a fly who has just walked into the spider's web after I tell you. I had called you earlier to ask if you would help type a paper for me but I certainly don't expect you to at this late notice."

"When is the paper due?"

"Tommorrow."

"How are you going to get it done?"

I pointed to my typewriter.

"Give me a chance to eat and come on over."

"But Tim, I couldn't do..."

"It would take you all night yourself wouldn't it?"

"Well...yeah...but you've got plans I'm sure and this will take a few hours even for the computer."

"That's okay. I don't mind. See you soon."

Shortly after 2 a.m. the paper was finished. What I didn't know until we were working on the paper was that Tim had to be at work early the next morning.

Tim didn't have to help but he did with no thought about himself. He put his own concerns on the shelf for a few hours to help me out of a tight spot. To me, that is real friendship. I was a friend in need and Tim was a friend indeed.

It reminds me of Proverbs 17:17 "A friend loves at all times..."

That's why I'm so thankful Jesus is my friend. I can relate to that. He said He was a friend day in and day out, in good and bad times, and available any time anywhere. He's there to listen and hurt with me or laugh with me. He understands my feelings when others don't even know there's a problem, and maybe I don't fully understand either. And he said nothing can separate us - time, distance, people — nothing. What a friend we have in Jesus.

"No in all things we are more than conquerors through Him who loved us. For I am sure that neither death, nor life, nor angels, nor principalities, nor things present, nor things to come, nor powers, nor height, nor depth, nor anything else in all creation will be able to separate us from the love of God in Christ Jesus our Lord" (Romans 8:37-39).

5

The Prodigal Son

Scripture: Luke 15:11-32

The boy felt like a battle was raging inside him. He loved his father but felt like he was missing something. He wanted to be with people his own age. So, he told his father he wanted his inheritance now and not later. The father had said "no" to several of his son's requests in the past. Like when he wanted to go swimming alone or build a fire too close to the house or have a wild animal for a pet.

But the father knew it would do no good to argue this time. Being a wise father, he gave him the money. It was hard for him to give the son half of what it took a *lifetime* to earn. He knew his son. He knew how the money would be spent. And yet he gave it to him.

The son used the money on wild and loose living. He had plenty of friends and girlfriends. But a funny thing happened. When his money ran out, so did his friends. Not one of those so-called friends helped him when he was hungry.

When he began thinking the pigs' food looked tasty, the young man "came to himself." What do you think that meant? _____

_____

He decided to go home and ask his father if he could work as a hired hand. He probably practiced how he would phrase it the whole way back home. After all, he had just wasted half

of his father's wealth and now was coming back to ask for *more* help. Maybe he also was thinking about his friends who turned out not to be his friends. Why could he not see that earlier? _____
_____

He could not see that his friends were using him. Why is that easy to do? _____
_____

Meanwhile, his father had looked down that road every day since his son had left. He loved him so much and prayed for him often. On this day, he saw someone walking down the road and thought, "That reminds me of my son." Then he recognized the familiar walk. "That *IS* my son!" He could not wait for him to get there and *ran* to meet him. He threw his arms around him and kissed him.
The son immediately tried to explain, using his carefully rehearsed words, "Father, I've sinned against heaven and you. I'm no longer worthy to be called your son." But the father was just happy his son was back and was too busy arranging a celebration to hear him. When the older brother asked why, the father explained, "Because your brother was dead and now is alive! He was lost and is now found!"

How is the son's father like God? _____
_____

How does that affect your life? _____
_____

The son's friends were not really his friends. They were using him. Does this happen today? _____ If so, how? _____
_____
_____

How can you tell if a friend is really a friend? _____
_____
_____

Sam's father suggested that they go camping together next weekend. Sam knew this was something special his father was doing for him. But next weekend was also Mary Stan-

ford's party. All of his friends would be there. What should Sam do? _____
_____

Mary felt left out by many of her friends. She felt like her friends did not like her for who she was and she needed to somehow win their friendship. What is wrong with Mary's logic?_____
_____

As a class, discuss this situation: Chris' friends participated in some things he did not want to do. But he was also afraid that he might be left out or rejected for not joining in. What would you do? _____
_____

Why is this a hard decision for Chris? _____
_____

What are some suggestions or helps Chris needs? (Write these on a poster and find a place to put it up in the room.)

Teacher instructions: Get a poster and some markers before class.

6

The Golden Rule in Dating

Scripture: Mark 12:28-34

Michael looked at the phone. How could anything so small look so scary? He reached for the receiver then quickly withdrew his arm. Today was the day and he knew it. He had already let Monday and Tuesday slip by and if he did not ask Angela out today, *right now*, his chances were practically gone. It was the unwritten code of the school that if you had not asked someone for a date by Wednesday, they probably would not go out with you on the weekend. Anything past Wednesday looked too much like a second choice or a desperation move.

Michael reached for the phone. This time he was going to do it. Just as he reached for the phone, it rang. Scared him to death, like a bolt of electricity had just gone through him. After about the third ring, he regained enough composure to answer.

"Hello."

"Michael?"

"Hey Drew!"

"What did Angela say?"

"Well, I haven't called her. I was just about to when you called."

"Sure. That's what you said yesterday and the day before. You better get with it. Today *is* Wednesday."

"I know. Say Drew, why don't you ask someone to go to the ball game too?"

"Are you kidding? My ego's fragile enough already. It couldn't take another 'I'd love to Drew, but I have other plans already.' "

"Okay. Well, I better call her before I lose my nerve."

"Good luck! I can't believe you're doing this!"

Michael started dialing Angela's number. His heart felt like the entire percussion section of the school band. He rehearsed what he was going to say . . . The phone started to ring. Michael started to sweat.

Asking a girl out for the first time was always hard for Michael. He had been out with girls before, but he usually knew them better than he knew Angela. Unfortunately, he and Angela had no classes together and really no mutual friends. They passed each other in the halls at school and said "Hi" but that was about it. He knew there had to be a better way to get to know Angela better, but he could not think of any.

The phone quit ringing and a deep male voice said, "Hello?"

Horror of horrors! It was her father! Michael cleared his throat and prayed his voice did not crack.

"May I speak to Angela please?"

"Certainly."

The second crawled by. Michael could feel his heart edging up toward his throat. His palms were cold and sweaty. And then,

"Hello?"

"Hi Angela. This is Michael Landers."

"Hi Michael."

They talked for a minute about school, classes and homework and then, "Angela, I was wondering if you'd like to go to the ball game with me Friday night?"

There was silence on the other end of the phone.

"Here it comes," Michael thought. "I knew I shouldn't have asked her. *Why* do I do these things?"

Angela broke the obvious pause. "Yes, Michael, I'd love to."

Michael was so excited he almost hung up. As soon as he finished his conversation with Angela, he quickly dialed Drew.

"Drew! It's Michael."

"I know who it is. Well, did you or didn't you?"

"I did."

"What's the verdict? Or should I say what's the excuse?"

"No excuse."

"Angela said yes?! I can't believe it!"

The next day as Michael and Drew were eating lunch at school, Drew looked past Michael's ham sandwich across the cafeteria.

"Michael, guess who's heading towards our table?"

Michael quickly straightened his cellophane, wiped his mouth and turned around. There stood Angela.

"Michael, could I speak to you for a minute?"

"Sure, have a seat."

"Well, I meant . . . maybe out in the hall."

Drew took his cue, "Hey I was just leaving. Why don't you talk here. It's dangerous out there with people running toward the cafeteria for food. I'll see you in class, Michael."

Michael did not feel too good. He was afraid of what he would hear from Angela. He looked at her across the table and smiled but inside his ham sandwich was churning.

"Michael, I know you'll hate me for this. But when I told you I'd go with you to the ball game, I forgot that my family was going out of town to my grandmother's this weekend. I'm really sorry, but I hope you'll understand."

Michael looked at her pleading face. He forced a smile and said he understood . . . He was in shock for the rest of the day. He felt like everybody who saw him knew Angela backed out of their date. Drew made no jokes about Angela. He knew that Michael was upset.

"Why don't you go to the game anyway, Michael. I'll be your date. I'll even buy the popcorn and shut my own car door."

"You're a scream Drew. Just hilarious. But maybe the game *would* put me in a better mood."

As a matter of fact it did . . . until he saw Angela walk into the gym . . . with Bubba Billers. Drew had spotted them too. "Michael, do you see who I see?"

"Yep."

Michael was floored. Emotions raced through him . . . embarrassment, anger, humiliation. He felt like crawling under the bleachers where nobody could see him. He felt like everyone knew what had happened and was watching him.

"Can you believe that?" Drew asked. "Bubba doesn't even look like Angela's grandmother. Hey Michael, I'm sorry this had to happen."

"It didn't have to happen. That's what I get for doing something stupid."

"Hey, it's not your fault," Drew said through a mouth full of popcorn. "You didn't know this was going to happen."

"Sure I did, Drew. I planned this whole thing so I could be publicly humiliated. I can't believe Angela would do this. Come on, let's go. I've seen enough."

Drew knew Michael was mad and opted for silence.

As they were leaving, Michael felt a hand on his shoulder. There was Angela.

"Michael, I'd like to talk for a minute."

Michael nodded and left Drew with his mouth hanging open. They walked outside and Michael sat down on the top step to the gym. He felt his body trembling. He was not sure if it was from anger or because he was about to cry.

Angela stood in front of him, a few steps down. "I know you're really mad at me . . . I lied to you about going to my grandmother's house. But I was hoping Bubba would ask me out this weekend. As a matter of fact, I thought when you called it might be Bubba. Anyway, I didn't think Bubba was going to ask me out, but when he did, I came up with a story about going to my grandmother's house. I wouldn't blame you if you never speak to me again. But believe it or not, I feel bad and wanted to tell you that I'm sorry."

Michael had been looking at Angela dead center. "Well, you're right, Angela. You did a terrible thing. You lied to me and embarrassed me in front of all those people in there. I asked you out because I thought it'd be fun to know you. Boy, are we having fun. I wish you had told me the truth in the first place."

Angela's big brown eyes filled with tears. Michael continued.

"I don't deserve to be treated like this. The way I want to be treated and try to treat others is with honesty. Now, Bubba's waiting on you and Drew has probably passed out."

"Michael, I'm sorry. Could you forgive me? What do you say? Friends?" Angela asked as she held out her hand.

"Angela, I'm trying very hard to be nice but it's not easy. I'm going to hear about this for the next two months at school. You're one of the prettiest girls I've ever met. But I don't want to go out with you, next week or next month."

"But you said ---"

"Listen, if I used the same lines you've said tonight, I hope somebody would tell me that I was still playing a game."

Angela's hand had long since dropped. Tears were streaming down her face. She walked past him and opened the door to go back inside.

"But," Michael said while still sitting on the top step. He held his hand up in the air. In a second, he felt two hands grab it from behind. "I would like for us to be friends. *Real* friends."

"You would?" he heard Angela sob from behind him.

"Honest."

Was this a realistic ending? _____ Why or why not? ____

What was Angela's mistake(s)? _____

What would you have done if you were Angela during Michael's phone call? _____
_____

Did Michael make a mistake(s)? If so, what? _____
_____
_____

Does self-image play a part in dating? _____ If so, how? __
_____
_____

How does Mark 12:28-34 apply to dating? _____
_____
_____

How does being a Christian affect your dating principles? __
_____
_____

How does the opinion of others affect who you go out with?
_____
_____

What do you look for in a boyfriend/girlfriend? _____
_____
_____

Divide into groups and write down the problems of dating:

Problems of Dating:
1)_____
2)_____
3)_____
4)_____
5)_____

Now reassemble as a class and share the problems and as a group, discuss solutions to these problems. Do not forget Mark 12:28-34 in deciding how to deal with these problems.

Solutions to the Problems of Dating:
1)_____
2)_____
3)_____

How to Love Others as Yourself
Keeping Christianity Alive in Relationships

1. Tell him/her if you do not want to go out with him/her. Honesty is the best policy.
2. Treat others with kindness and fairness.
3. Don't be afraid to ask the girl out. But respect her decision not to go out with you. Girls, respect the boy for asking.
4. End relationships with kindness and courtesy.
5. You must like yourself before you can expect anyone else to.
6. You must respect yourself before you can expect anyone else to. You have to be an individual and stand by your beliefs, regardless of what others may do or think.
7. Set your guidelines and standards *before* you date, not as you go along.
8. You need Christian friends who will encourage and support your actions.
9. Dating someone who is not a Christian is very hard. You will usually change more than he/she does. Evangelism is more effective between friends than girlfriends and boyfriends.
10. You are an individual made by God and must trust that He knows best for your life, even with your girlfriend or boyfriend.

7

Daniel and the Lions' Den

Scriptures: Daniel 6:1-23; Matthew 5:13-16

King Darius made a law for *everyone* to pray only to him or be killed. Daniel had always prayed to God. When he heard (and saw) that *everyone else* was praying to the king, Daniel had a decision to make: go along with everyone else or suffer the consequences.

You have decisions to make too: *go along with everyone else or suffer the consequences.* In this case the consequences were a horrible death. What are some ways you decide to differ from others? _____
_____

What are some consequences?_____
_____

Daniel gave thanks to God, not Darius, and was put in a room with lions. God delivered Daniel. No mark was found on him "because he trusted in God." Was this a hard decision for Daniel to make? _____ Explain: _____
_____

Today you also have decisions to make. It is a lot easier to do what everyone else is doing. You want them to like you. You want their acceptance and approval. Yet you also know you should not participate in some of the things everyone else is doing. Jesus tells us we cannot serve two masters (Matthew 6:24). How does this apply to peer pressure? _____

Jill is in the car with her date and two other couples. One of the other couples suggest that they stop for a beer. What should Jill do? _____

Josh really wants to be accepted. He does not feel too good about himself. He knows he does some silly things sometimes just to get attention. A person that Josh really wants to like him asks him to do something Josh considers to be wrong.

What is Josh's problem? _____

What should Josh do? _____

How do friends influence our actions -- right or wrong? ___

Read Matthew 5:13-16.

What does God want for us in life? He wants us to seek His kingdom, to trust Him and to be a light for Him. But what is our reaction? Too often we head in exactly the opposite direction! We see how far we can get to wrong without actually sinning. Draw a vertical line in the middle of the space below. To the left of the line write SIN. To the right, write GOOD.

You want to stay in the GOOD area, but you are often tempted to see how close you can get to that line without going across it. The problem with that is that you are heading in the wrong direction! Instead of seeing how much *good* we can do, too often we are more concerned about how close we can get to that line. Right?

Part of the problem has to do with the way you feel about yourself. You may do things that you know are wrong to gain acceptance of others. You may not feel like they can accept you for who you are and so you have to show you are worthy. Another part of the problem is our lack of trust in God. Do you put that trust into action in facing daily temptations?

With the person sitting next to you, list five tips for trusting God:

1)_____
2)_____
3)_____
4)_____
5)_____

Divide into two groups. Each group should come up with a realistic situation which calls for a decision (similar to Josh and Jill's situations). Write the situation down. Then exchange situations with the other group. Decide how your group would react to the situation and share your responses with the other group.

⚬⧫⚬⧫⚬⧫⚬

Teacher instructions: You will need some paper and pencils. Perhaps you will want to come up with more situations for the students to deal with. If so, write them on slips of paper, fold them up, put them in a container and let each group choose a slip of paper.

8

Joseph: Trusting in God

Scripture: Genesis 37:1-4,12-28; 39:1-23

Joseph suffered terrible injustices for serving God. List a few of them:
1)_____
2)_____
3)_____
4)_____
5)_____

Divide into groups and determine what a modern day parallel to Joseph's situations would be.
_____
_____
_____

Is it possible for *you* to suffer for serving God? _____
Please explain. _____
_____
_____

What are some of the "ingredients" of Joseph's faith?
1)_____
2)_____
3)_____
4)_____
5)_____

What are some ways to deal with temptations? _____
_____
_____

How can God help you fight temptations? _____
_____
_____

When do you let Him help you and when is it difficult to trust Him? _____
_____
_____

Remember, Joseph did not know what would happen to him when he was sold into slavery or put in prison. He received no special treatment just because he would later be included in Genesis 39. (No one said, "Hey, isn't that Joseph, that famous biblical character from the book of Genesis?") But he trusted in God and God "was with" Joseph (Genesis 39:21).

Is God with you as He was with Joseph? _____ Please explain. _____
_____

As a class, discuss ways that you trust God. _____
_____

Solomon tried to find happiness and security in several things before recognizing it was like trying to grab hold of the wind. You have that same temptation. What are some things you are tempted to put your trust in?
1)_____
2)_____
3)_____
4)_____
5)_____

Take a look at each of these and decide the weakness in placing your trust in them.

Trust Situations*

What "trust situations" did you come up with?_____
_____

Thoughts during demonstration of trust: _____
_____
_____

Thoughts about how you trust God: _____
_____
_____

What everyday situations require trust in God for you? ___
_____
_____

How can you increase your trust in God? _____
_____
_____

*Teacher instructions:
1) Have the class participate in thinking of trust situations (example -- trusting the pilot on your flight).
2) Plan a way that trust can be demonstrated in the classroom (example -- a student falling backwards with his eyes closed into another's arms).

3) Discuss how this trust relates to our trust in God and how much trust we actually give God.

"FACING DISAPPOINTMENTS"

I've been thinking about tests Christians face. A hard one for me is facing disappointment. Let me give you an example. You try as hard as you can to make the football team. You lift weights all summer and jog two miles every day. A day doesn't go by that you don't picture yourself on the football starting team. And yet when the team roster is posted you see that your name is not on it. You didn't make the team. How do you handle your disappointment?

Or suppose you study hard for a test and still make a low score? What is your reaction? What if you didn't make the cheerleading squad? What if you're not asked to join the National Honor Society? What if you can't find an after school job?

Picture this: the score is tied, there are two outs in the last inning and you're up to bat with a full count. The next pitch is obviously outside but the umpire calls it "Striiike Three!" Do you throw down your helmet and stomp out on the field? Or what if that "special someone" doesn't think you're so special? How do you deal with that? How do you cope when things go all wrong? When you are embarrassed or hurt or mad?

Maybe you've experienced milder but still painful forms of disappointment. Perhaps you made the team, but sit on the bench. Maybe you made a B on your report card when you thought you were going to get an A. Or you were invited to a party, but didn't enjoy it very much. A more discreet type of disappointment is that while nothing bad happened to you at school today, nothing good did either. What is your reaction? This is a test for the Christian. How we handle situations when things go sour tests our commitment to be God's person. Do you know what I'm talking about? Let's say you don't make the cheerleading squad. How might you be tempted to respond? In a word, rotten. That's the time that it may be hardest for you to be God's person. I know a girl who wanted very badly to be a cheerleader. Most of her friends were cheerleaders, and she wanted to share in the excitement. Three times she tried out and three times she didn't make it. Each time she was hurt and disappointed. Each time when she got home the night after the election, she cried-no sobbed for hours. That's pain. She knows what disappointment is all about.

Disappointment poses challenge to our Christian lifestyle. I have some suggestions for you on how to face disappointment.

1). **It's not a sin to feel disappointment.** Matter of fact, it's better to admit to yourself and to your friends that you are disappointed and explain why. That way you've explained your unusual behavior to your friends (after all they might think you're mad at them), you've admitted it to yourself (that might help you monitor your behavior and insure that you don't take it out on your brother or sister), and you've given your friends an opportunity to provide support. That leads to the second point.

2). **Allow your friends to help.** They can and will. You'll soon learn that they like you even when you don't feel so great about yourself. This leads to number 3.

3). **Realize that disappointment causes you to feel bad about yourself.** It lowers your self image. Remember, we all fail. The tragedy is not in failing, but being afraid to try. Pick yourself up, dust yourself off and get back in there! You can't always succeed, but you can learn from your mistakes. On to number 4.

4). **Learn from your disappointment.** Perhaps you need to study differently for a test. Maybe you need to try another sport. Also, if you said some things you didn't mean in the agony of disappointment, don't repeat your mistake again. Learn to anticipate disappointment by asking yourself how should you react to disappointment.

5). **Be a good loser.** People look to see how you respond to disappointment. It helps your light shine or extinguishes it. If you lose, accept it graciously. People remember the way you accept disappointment. For example, what's John Macenroe remembered for? His victories over Borg? His numerous championship titles? No-the way he handles his disappointment.

It's hard to accept disappointment in a way which pleases God. It takes practice and a strong allegiance to God's principles.

9

Shadrach, Meshach and Abednego

Scripture: Daniel 3:1-30

Have you ever known anyone who thought he (she) was *it*? You know, a person who thinks the world revolves around him. Everything he says begins with "I" and ends with "me." He never seems to have time to talk about you. Sometimes it is easy to feel more important than you really are. King Nebuchadnezzar had that very problem. He was the king of Babylon, the most powerful nation on earth at the time. Wouldn't it be easy to *feel* important if you were the king of the most powerful nation in the world? You might think *you* were the most important person on earth.

What can make a person feel "too" important? _____
_____

Therefore, it is not hard to understand why King Nebuchadnezzar started thinking about building an image of gold. This was no ordinary image of gold. This image was nine feet wide and ninety feet tall! It was built on the Plain of Dura. We are not sure if the image was actually in the shape of Nebuchadnezzar, but it was created to honor him.

Finally the dedication day arrived. The king sent invitations to "everybody that was anybody" to come. So they all came and stood before the image. What an impressive looking crowd that must have been. A Who's Who of Babylon.

So there was Nebuchadnezzar on his platform overlooking the people. A herald gave these instructions to the people:

"Everybody needs to listen to what I'm about to say. It's a matter of life and death. You are commanded to bow to the image when you hear the orchestra begin and anyone who fails to bow will be thrown into the furnace." Although we are not positive, chances are this furnace was used to burn the city's garbage. Then the time came. The orchestra began to play and all of the people went down on their knees. This must have made Nebuchadnezzar very proud to look out and see all of these important people bowing to his image.

Do you think the people liked Nebuchadnezzar? Why? ____
_____

Is being popular enough? _____ Why? _____
_____
_____

It was at this time that certain Chaldeans came up to Nebuchadnezzar and said, "Oh King, live forever. Remember, King, that you decreed that everyone should bow

down and worship the golden image and whoever doesn't will be thrown into the furnace? Well, Shadrach, Meshach and Abednego are paying no attention to your command."

King Nebuchadnezzar was furious and commanded that they be brought to him. Then he asked if they refused to worship the image and told them he was going to give them another chance. After all, they might have been in the back of the crowd and could not hear the instructions or the orchestra. Nebuchadnezzar said something to this effect, "In just a second the orchestra will strike up again and you'll be able to show your allegiance to me in front of all these people by bowing before the golden image. If you fall down to the image, good, but if you don't, even though I've set you in high places, you'll be thrown into the burning furnace. And who is the god that will deliver you out of my hands?"

A tight spot to be in. What would you have done if you were in their place? _____
_____

It is easy for us to take for granted the faith of these three because we know the outcome. But, these men did not know what was going to happen. Their reply was that they trusted in God to deliver them, but if He chose not to, they would remain faithful to Him. They would not serve any other god, and that went for the big one behind them.

What are your "Nebuchadnezzars" today? _____
_____

As you might imagine, this made Nebuchadnezzar mad. The Bible says that the expression on his face was changed against these men. He ordered that the furnace be heated as hot as possible. Shadrach, Meshach and Abednego were tied and were led by the strongest men in the army to the furnace. The fire was so hot, it killed the men who pushed them in. Again, remember, for all Shadrach, Meshach and Abednego knew, they were about to face a very painful death. Even though they may have been scared, they remained faithful. How does that compare with:

Job _____
Stephen _____

Peter _____
Jesus _____
Moses _____

But Shadrach, Meshach and Abednego were not killed. King Nebuchadnezzar rose in haste and asked, "Didn't we cast three men tied up in the fire? But I see *four* men *walking* in the middle of the fire, unhurt!"

The king and all the people later discovered Shadrach, Meshach and Abednego were unharmed and did not even smell like smoke. Nebuchadnezzar then said, "Blessed be the God of Shadrach, Meshach and Abednego who has sent His angel and delivered His servants *who trusted in Him and risked their lives in trusting their God* rather than serving my idol."

The king went from trying to kill these men to promoting them and commanding that his nation honor *their* God. Now the chances of you being thrown into a furnace are slim. But, how are decisions you make similar to the decision these men had to make? _____
_____
_____

Is it easier to die for God or live for Him? _____
Explain. _____
_____

What are some fates we consider "worse than death"? ____
_____
_____

Put these scriptures into your own words:
2 Corinthians 5:1,6,7 _____
_____

2 Corinthians 8:1-5 _____
_____

Write down or tell of a situation in which you put your trust in God instead of what someone else was doing or asked you to do. _____
_____
_____

Shadrach, Meshach and Abednego trusted God with their lives. God asks us to do the same thing. You make choices every day of where to put your trust . . . in areas like honesty, friendship, dating, language, obedience and kindness. A central issue concerns your willingness to trust God with your life. I believe that God is just as proud of you when you trust Him as He was of Shadrach, Meshach and Abednego that day on the Plain of Dura.

Teacher instructions: Use your imagination in presenting the story of Shadrach, Meshach and Abednego. You may wish to use visual aids (chalkboard, overhead projectors, etc.). Have the dimensions of Nebuchadnezzar's golden image calculated on something you can show the students during class (like a tree or a building or a piece of string).

As for the question about "fates worse than death," you might also ask for the every day things considered as fates worse than death. For example: "having to go to school with dirty hair."

10
Job

Scriptures: Job 1:1-5,13-22; 2:7-10; 42:12-16; Matthew 5:3; 11:28-30

Let us pretend that you are asleep in your bed tonight and a little fairy awakens you with her wand and grants you three wishes. What will you wish for?
1)_____
2)_____
3)_____

How is God different from a fairy? _____
_____

Do you treat Him differently? Please explain: _____
_____
_____

What does poor in spirit mean (Matthew 5:3)? Someone who doesn't have much faith? That's what it sounds like. But it means exactly the opposite. This verse is saying, "Blessed are those who realize their *need* for God." Sometimes when things are going well, it's easy to think you don't need God. For example, you feel happy, things are going just how you want them to go, so you don't feel like you need God too much. What else could he do that I don't already have? What's wrong with this kind of thinking?_____
_____

Job trusted in God in good times and bad, even when his friends and family tried to change his mind. Name three qualities about Job you would like to have.

1)_____
2)_____
3)_____

In Matthew 11:28-30, Jesus asks that you give Him your "burdens." What type of burdens was He talking about? ____
_____

The word Jesus used for "burden" was understood by the people He was talking to. They used the word all the time. It is the same word used to describe weights people and animals physically carried. In the narrow streets of Jerusalem, donkeys were used to carry heavy packages. In an effort to avoid making several trips, the owner would double or triple the weight on the donkey. Sometimes a donkey would collapse under all that weight in the middle of the

street. So when Jesus said to come to Him with burdens, the people understood. Why is this good news for you 2000 years later? _____
_____

Is Matthew 11:28-30 a hard command to obey? _____ Why? _____
_____

John Walker had a lot of things going his way. He made good grades, was well liked, had a good family, his own car, and was getting along great with his girlfriend. But somehow, John did not feel too spiritual. He seldom prayed, except when he needed help, and never read his Bible. He knew he should but just could not get motivated.
Why? _____
_____

What would you say to John? _____
_____

Job evidently had everything going his way too. And yet his attitude toward God was different even before tragedy struck. Why? _____
_____

What is the difference between people like Job and John?___
_____

Lynn had studied for days for the chemistry exam. But when she received the test, she forgot some of the answers. She noticed that a few of her friends were cheating when the teacher left the room. She realized their scores would be higher than hers and possibly raise the "curve." She knew she should not cheat, but she was beginning to panic. Why is this a hard decision? _____
_____

What should Lynn do? _____
_____

How is this a decision of whether to trust God or not? _____
_____

What is the hardest for you to trust God with? _____

How can you daily trust God more? _____

Teacher instructions: This lesson allows you to break some of the class time into groups. The situations and questions on John and Lynn would allow for this. Additional questions to bring up could be:
When do you pray?
What do you pray for?
How can you make your prayer life better?

11

The Rich Young Ruler

Scriptures: Matthew 19:16-24; Luke 18:18-24; Mark 10:17-25

We know the story of the rich young ruler by heart. He asks Jesus what he needs to do to inherit eternal life. Why did he ask? No one really knows. Perhaps it was to get Jesus to say, "You don't need to do anything else. I just wish more people were like you!" Or *maybe he felt like something was missing even though he was obeying all the rules.* Jesus answered by saying not to commit adultery, not to murder, not to steal and honor your mother and father, and the man said, "I've obeyed these commandments ever since I was a child." (At this point we are saying, "Oh yeah? Well just wait 'til this next question!")

Jesus looked at the man and had compassion on him. He loved him. He looked him in the eye and said, "There is one more thing. Sell everything you have and give it to the poor." The young man went away crushed. He could not do it. Wonder how Jesus felt watching that man walk away? _____

Meanwhile we are shaking our heads and wisely saying, "He put something in front of God. That is what happens when you stop putting your life in God's hands."

Don't misunderstand. I think we can learn a lot from others' mistakes. But . . . I don't think we should be too quick to criticize this fellow. For example, have *you* ever considered something more important than God? Sure you have. Several times. For example:

Have you cheated on a test? You put your grades before God.

Have you ever ridiculed someone else? You put your cruel words before God's instructions.

Have you ever lied to your parents? You put your wisdom above God's.

Have you ever treated someone in a less than kind way? You put your concerns above God's.

Jesus told the man it was well and good that he was keeping the commandments. But Jesus wanted *HIM*. His heart, his life. A commitment that would let nothing be more important than His Father.

> Describe a modern day Rich Young Ruler: _____
> _____

Steve and Jerry are the best of friends. They both want to be in a social club. However, the fraternity asked Jerry and not Steve to join. Jerry has a decision to make. He really wants to be in the club but he has some misgivings about being in a club that would not take his best friend. What should Jerry do? _____
_____

Why? _____
_____

Why do we sometimes consider other things more important than God? _____
_____

Can you think of examples in the Bible in which a person or people put something or someone else before God? _____
1) _____
2) _____
3) _____

Read either Matthew 6:19-24 or Mark 4:35-40 and explain how the passage deals with your trust in God: _____
_____
_____

How are you sometimes like the Rich Young Ruler?_____

Christianity involves more than going to Sunday school class, worship services and occasional visits to the nursing homes. God wants your undivided allegiance. There can be only one master. Trying to live like God wants you to and at the same time doing things that are wrong is like being in the middle of a tug-of-war. It can tear you apart.

Name at least two ways you can put God first this week:
1)_____
2)_____

Teacher instructions: Put these ways the students are going to put God first this week on a poster and hang it up in the room. At the beginning of next week's class, call attention to the poster and ask the students to evaluate how they did.

You might also ask the students to write their two ways on a sheet of paper, seal them in an envelope you provide, address them and turn them in to you. In turn, you can mail them about mid-week as an encouragement to them to keep their commitment.

12

The Good Samaritan

Scripture: Luke 10:25-37

Jesus was asked by an expert in the scriptures, "What must I do to inherit eternal life?" Jesus asked him what the law said and the expert replied with two passages, "Love the Lord your God with all your soul and with all your strength and with all your mind" (Deuteronomy 6:5), and "Love your neighbor as yourself" (Leviticus 19:18). His answer showed he had studied the scriptures about this question. Jesus said he had answered correctly and said, "Do this and you will live."

But this man was asking questions to trap Jesus. So he asked another question, "And who is my neighbor?" To answer Jesus told of a man traveling from Jerusalem to Jericho. He was robbed, beaten, stripped of his clothes and left on the side of the road, half dead.

A priest happened to come down the road and crossed to the other side, passing the man by. Another man, a Levite, saw him ahead and also crossed to the other side and passed by. Then a man from Samaria saw the man and helped him. He took care of his cuts, put him on his donkey and took him to an inn where he watched after him that night. The next day, he gave the innkeeper money in advance for the man's expenses, asked him to take care of him and promised to pay for any additional expense.

We don't know if the Samaritan was wealthy or poor, in a hurry like the other two or anything else about him. We don't know how far away the inn was, if it was out of his way or if he had to walk while the man rode where he had been riding. riding.

Jesus asked the question, "Who of the three men was a neighbor?" The expert replied, "The one who had mercy on him." Jesus answered to go and do likewise.

> How does the Good Samaritan apply to the way you treat others? _____
>
> How does the Good Samaritan apply to the way you treat your family? _____

Ann Horn was the new kid in school. Her family had moved to town in the middle of the year. Nobody went out of their way to be mean to Ann, but nobody could be accused of being too friendly to her either. She went home in tears the first day because she had no friends.

Bob Wallace noticed that Ann sat alone in the cafeteria and did not seem to have any friends yet. He wanted to help her feel more at home but didn't know quite what to do. But he knew if he did *anything*, everyone would tease him.

What can Bob do? _____

What are some reasons for not accepting new people? _____

How does the story of being a neighbor help in reaching out to people you do not know? _____

How Will You Be Remembered?

I guarantee that I know two subjects you think about a lot. Believe me? OK, see if I am right. Number One: you think about "that special someone," you know, your boyfriend or girlfriend or whomever you wish were your boyfriend or girlfriend. Number Two is your friends. You want them to like you. You want them to save you a seat in the cafeteria, on the bus or at the game. You want them to enjoy your company, not dread it.

How did I do on my predictions? No, I am not Carnak or even the Amazing Kreskin. Those are just normal thoughts for teenagers to have. In other words, all *those other* kids at your school, band, team, church or rink have those same thoughts and even worries! The very people you hope like you, hope you will like them. Of course, not *everyone* that you would like to date or do things with will what to do things with you. You've probably already found that out, huh?

I had an experience the other day that brought some of these things together and I'd like to share it with you. About a month ago, I went to my ten-year class reunion. Now take a look at your best friends and imagine what they will look like in ten years! That is exactly what I had to do. I dusted off the old annual and looked at the photos of my classmates and tried to imagine what they would look like ten years later. It was like a trip into Fantasy Island, only it was real.

But here is the real surprise -- everyone was asked to tell *what they remembered* most about high school. Of course some wrote about funny things that happened, but guess what most people wrote? Memories like "I remember my first week of school back in the 9th grade. I was so nervous, I cried every day. But Vicki and Sharon became my friends and invited me to eat with them in the cafeteria and I've never forgotten it!" That was 14 years ago! Many recalled acts of kindness and indications of acceptance.

I was surprised. I should not have been. Those were the kinds of memories I had too. Somehow, I thought there would be more emphasis on the football or cheerleading activities. Does my experience say anything to you about your current relationships? It says to me they aren't going to remember if you dropped the winning touchdown pass. They probably won't even remember that you were on the team. They won't remember the clothes you wear or the car you drive. They won't remember who won which award. If they won't remember it, it probably doesn't impress them too much.

You do not have to be on the team or in the band to earn someone's friendship. A friendship on that basis is not much of a friendship. So what *will* your friends remember? How you treat them. If you had time for them. If you used them. If you

treated them with respect. If you were a friend when they really needed one. Here is something else I learned. You know those people that you make fun of, that everyone makes jokes about? They have memories too and they attend ten-year reunions and they usually surprise people because they are attorneys or doctors or teachers. Jesus called some of them "the least of these" in Matthew 25 and said the way we treat them is the way we treat Him.

Do you want to be appreciated by your friends? Follow the advice of Jesus in Matthew 7 and treat them the way that you would want to be treated.

Treating others in an unkind way never helps your cause. Even when others hurt you, treat them with respect. Take time to talk to the class scapegoat, the one everybody likes to make jokes about it. Help others, with no secret motive. Be a friend just to be a friend, not to use someone. Believe me, you will not only have more quality relationships now, but it will make your ten-year reunion much easier to attend!

> Imagine that you and your classmates are having a ten-year class reunion. Ten years from now how do you want to be remembered?

*Teacher instructions: It might be interesting for the students to individually work through the exercises and questions about Ann and Bob. Have the students spread out in the classroom. Afterwards, discuss their responses and read the article together.

13

The Salt of the Earth

Scripture: Matthew 5:14-16; 25:31-46

Relate an example of how your actions revealed that you were a Christian. _____
_____
_____

If you will, share your example with the class.

List three people in the Bible who made it clear to others that they were serving God.
1) _____
2) _____
3) _____

List three adults you consider "lights."
1) _____
2) _____
3) _____

> Apply Matthew 25:31-46 in your own words.
> Example: "For I needed someone to talk to and you listened."
> For I _____
> and you _____
> For I _____
> and you _____
> Why is this scripture sometimes hard to obey? _____

Where is it hard/easy to obey Matthew 25:31-46?
Place an H or E in each of the blanks. If you have trouble deciding, you can use H/E or a ?.

____ Home   ____ Church
____ School   ____ On a date
____ When you're mad   ____ When you're happy
____ When you make a low grade
____ Other situations _____

Teacher instructions: Take the applications of Matthew 25 and get some of the class members to put them on a nice poster to hang in the room for next quarter or session.

How You Can be a Light *Even* When . . .

You strike out with the bases loaded?
You try out for cheerleading and do not make it?
A friend hurts your feelings?
You do not have a date on Friday night (and you wanted one!)?
Your little brother spills Elmer's glue all over your new shirt?
Your parents want you to stay home and you want to go out?
Some tragedies have happened in your life?
Things are going great?
You embarrass yourself?
You are mad?
You feel left out?
You feel scared?

Teacher's instructions for final exercise of the class:
"Being Lights for the Lord"

Cut some poster board up into 3" x 5" sizes. Write captions on them that indicate how a person in possession of the caption might be treated. For example, captions should be similar to: "I'M LIKABLE, AGREE WITH ME" or "I'M A NOBODY, IGNORE ME." Use your imagination to come up with captions different from these. Ask other teachers or a couple of students to help.

Fasten or tape these signs to about five caps or hats and pick out five students to wear these hats in class. The person wearing the cap should not know what his/her caption says. The students wearing the caps should sit in a semicircle facing the class and should conduct a conversation in which they treat each other as their caps instruct. That is, they would ignore the person wearing the "I'M A NOBODY, IGNORE ME" caption and agree with the person wearing the "I'M LIKABLE, AGREE WITH ME" caption. The rest of the students in the class should remain silent.

Discussion topics may include:
"My favorite color is _____ because _____."
"My favorite pet is _____ because _____."
"My favorite soft drink is _____ because _____."

After a few minutes of conversation, ask each participant to guess what his/her caption says.

Discuss the exercise with the class. How did each participant feel? How do we affect others? How are we like lights and salt as Jesus described in Matthew 5:14-16?